Dear
Man of God

LaToya Newson

www.TrueVinePublishing.org

Dear Man of God
LaToya Newson

Published by
True Vine Publishing Co.
810 Dominican Dr. Ste. 103
Nashville, TN. 37228
www.TrueVinePublishing.org

ISBN: 978-1-956469-87-5 Paperback
ISBN: 978-1-956469-91-2 eBook

Scripture quotations marked KJV are taken from the Holy Bible King James Version

Printed in the United States of America—First printing

Dedication

I dedicate this book to the men in my life—my husband, my son, my father, my brothers, my uncles, and countless cousins. Thank you for being men of integrity, honor, and valor. I am grateful for each of you and the impact you've had on my life.

You have taught me the true meaning of love and patience. You taught me how to survive and thrive in the midst of adversity. You have encouraged me to be the best version of myself and to live life abundantly. Thank you for loving me!

Table of Contents

Day 1:
Identity in Christ

Dear Man of God,

Despite what social media says or how you are portrayed in society, remember that you are fearfully and wonderfully made by the creator. God uniquely designs you for a specific purpose that only you can fulfill. In a world that often tries to fit people into boxes and categories based on race, upbringing, education, or lack thereof, God has designed you to be different and stand out amongst the crowd.

As a man, there is much pressure to conform to a unilateral image of masculinity. Society often defines masculinity by superficial standards, emphasizing power, dominance, and self-centeredness, but the true definition of a man is his willingness to conform to the image of Christ. Therefore, you are not limited to a narrow set of roles and traits. Instead, you are meant to mirror the characteristics of Christ Himself.

You are called to be a protector, just as Christ is the ultimate protector. Your physical, mental, and emotional strength can be used to create a safe and secure environment for those around you.

You are called to be a provider who positions yourself to receive from the provision of God following the example of Christ, who meets your every need.

You are called to be a lover, just as Christ loves unconditionally. Your love should extend beyond romantic relationships and encompass deep care and compassion for others. Love sacrificially, forgive readily, and extend grace abundantly. Let your actions and words reflect the love of Christ.

You are called to be a teacher, sharing wisdom and truth with those around you. As a man, you are privileged to lead and guide others, impart knowledge, and invest in the next generation. Seek wisdom from God's Word and let it shape your understanding and teaching.

Remember, you are multidimensional! You don't have to conform to societal expectations. Instead, look to the Word of God and put Christ as your example. Seek to align your thoughts, actions, and character with Jesus' standards. Embrace the unique qualities and strengths God has bestowed upon you, and use them for His glory.

SCRIPTURES:
Psalms 139:14, Ephesians 2:10

Take time today to reflect on the unique qualities God has given you as a man. List what gifts, talents, abilities, and characteristics make you unique, even what others call weird. You can even ask some of your friends and family. Then meditate on the scriptures above and read over your list, knowing that who you are is who God handcrafted you to be.

Journal

_____

_____

_____

_____

_____

_____

_____

_____

_____

_____

_____

_____

_____

_____

_____

_____

_____

_____

_____

_____

_____

_____

_____

_____

_____

_____

Day 2:
What Does It Mean to be A Man of God?

Dear Man of God,

What does being a man of God mean to you? When I think about those words and what Christ embodied, it means embracing love, understanding, perseverance, and having intimacy with the Creator.

To be a man of God means not being afraid to love. Men can be great lovers, but to love correctly and completely requires transparency. Vulnerability is not a sign of weakness but an act of humility that allows you to draw strength from God and let those you trust and care about have the opportunity to love you unconditionally. As you love others authentically without withholding, you emulate the love that God has lavished upon us. Love selflessly, sacrificially, and unconditionally, just as Jesus Christ loved you.

Being open to giving love starts with receiving love. When you understand how much God loves you, it helps you to trust his leadership. Being a man of God means seeking to understand what you don't know. It means humbly acknowledging when you don't have all the answers and being willing to learn and grow. When you remain open to receive instruction, God will speak, direct and send people to lead you in the right direction as you lead others because that is what love does.

As a man of God, you are the answer to the need.

Sometimes the most significant needs are outside the walls of the church. Be willing to go where the need is, extend a helping hand, lend a listening ear, and share the hope found in Jesus. Do not be afraid to show love or to receive it. Open your heart to the transformative power of God's love and allow it to flow through you to others.

Intimacy with the Creator is essential for a man of God. Take time to read and study God's Word, allowing it to transform your mind and heart. Then, as your faith in God grows, you will persevere in the face of fear, knowing that God is with you, increasing your ability to trust in His faithfulness and take courage in His promises.

To truly live out your identity as a man of God, you must do the work of knowing what God says about who you are. Dive deep into scripture, meditate on His promises, and seek His guidance. Discover the purpose and blessings God has given you since your creation.

SCRIPTURES:
Genesis 1:26-27, Genesis 2:15

Take some time to reflect on your relationship with God. Is it where you want it to be? If not, what changes can you make today to draw him closer to you?

Journal

Day 3:
Suffering in Silence

Dear Man of God,

You were not created to do life alone. One of the many tricks of the enemy is for us to go through challenges and believe that we are going through them alone, that we are the only ones facing difficult circumstances and trials. But the truth is, God never designed us to bear the weight of the world by ourselves. We were created for community. God confirmed this by saying in Genesis 2:18 that it is not good for man to be alone.

Contrary to popular belief, God does not expect us to be happy every single day. Happiness is a fickle circumstantial emotion that changes depending on your thoughts. Life is filled with ups and downs, joys, and challenges. You don't have to pretend you have it all together when you don't. It's okay not to be okay. The caveat is you do not have to stay in that place. Pretending life is grand only worsens the internal war. When you admit you are not okay, God can step in and do what you can't. You have a heavenly Father who is always ready to help you, and He has also placed people in your life who are assigned to support you.

Community is not just for the sunshine days when everything is going right. It's there to help you when it's raining, when darkness surrounds you, and when you feel alone. Don't underestimate the power of reaching out for

Dear Man of God

support. God doesn't heal who we pretend to be; He heals who we are. Just as you would not go to the doctor pretending that everything is okay when you're not feeling well, be honest with God and others about your struggles. It is in our vulnerability and honesty that help and healing show up.

Recognizing that seeking outside help is not a sign of weakness is essential. It's an act of strength and humility. Don't hesitate to contact a counselor, coach, or therapist if needed. Even the Bible describes Jesus as a wonderful counselor. God wants us to seek out help and not suffer in silence. A therapist can provide an objective viewpoint and a safe space to express your hurts and struggles.

Not every pastor is trained in therapeutic practices, and that's okay. It's important to seek help from someone licensed and trained to deal with specific issues. Just as you would go to a qualified dentist for a root canal, seek out professionals equipped to address your particular needs.

Remember, seeking therapy or counseling is not a sign of weakness but an act of courage and a pursuit of strength. It's an opportunity to grow, heal, and find wholeness in Christ.

SCRIPTURES:
1 Peter 5:7, Mathew 28:20, Ecclesiastes 4:9-10

Are there any struggles that you need to share or get help for? Find someone you trust or locate a professional and begin to open up about your struggles so you can find the support, freedom, and relief you need.

Journal

Day 4:
Freedom in Love

Dear Man of God,

I know we have talked about love, but let's talk about the different types of love and how they impact our lives. Love is a powerful force that goes far beyond the romantic relationships we often associate it with. Love drives us to serve others, wake up each day with purpose, and care for our families and children. It is not just something we live but also something we communicate.

Several types of love are described in the Bible, each with its own significance and expression. The first is "agape" love, which is unconditional and sacrificial love. This is the love that God has for us and that we are called to have for one another. It is a selfless love that seeks the well-being and welfare of others without expecting anything in return.

The second type of love is "philia" love, which refers to brotherly love or deep friendship. This is the love we have for our close friends and companions. It involves loyalty, trust, and mutual support. Philia love is vital to building strong relationships and fostering community.

Another type of love is "storge" love, which is the affectionate love within families. It is the love between parents and children, siblings, and extended family members. Storge love is characterized by care, nurturing, and a deep bond from shared experiences.

Lastly, there is "eros" love, which is the romantic and passionate love between a husband and wife. It involves desire, attraction, and intimacy. Eros love is a gift from God to be expressed within the bounds of marriage, creating a solid bond between spouses. As men of God, you are called to embody and express these different types of love. It should be evident in your dedication to your jobs, how you care for your families, and the love you show to your children.

Love is not just a feeling but an intentional choice and action. God wouldn't have sent Jesus to die for our sins if he loved us without action. Love acts and displays itself in practical ways; it is a powerful force that can transform lives and bring glory to God. My prayer for you today is that you choose to love today.

SCRIPTURES:
John 3:16 and Galatians 5:13

Take time today to reflect on the different types of love and how you can express them. Then, write down some ways to act in love and be more intentional about loving others.

Journal

_____

_____

_____

_____

_____

_____

_____

_____

_____

_____

_____

_____

_____

_____

_____

_____

_____

_____

_____

_____

_____

_____

_____

_____

_____

Day 5:
Operating with Integrity

Dear Man of God,

Integrity is the outward practice of inward belief; doing what is right even when no one is watching. It aligns your audio and video, ensuring harmonious words and actions.

Living and operating with integrity is crucial because it reflects the character of God in us. People can trust what we say and do when our words and actions align. It builds a foundation of credibility and reliability, which means that a lack of integrity leads to a lack of trust. Like watching movies with perfectly synchronized audio and video, others can have confidence in our character when our words and actions are in sync.

As men of God, you are called to live with integrity in every aspect of your lives. You are to honor God in public and in secret places where no one else sees. Your integrity should extend to your thoughts, choices, and behaviors. When faced with temptation, when no one is watching, you must consciously choose to do what is right.

Integrity is not about being perfect; it's about acknowledging our imperfections and continually striving to align our lives with the truth of God's Word. It means seeking forgiveness when we fall short and making amends when we have caused intentional or unintentional harm. It requires humility, honesty, and a sincere desire to

honor God in all that we do. When we put God at the fore-
front of all we do, integrity becomes a byproduct of God's
proper place in our life.

SCRIPTURES:
Proverbs 11:3 and Proverbs 21:3

Take time today to reflect on the areas of your life
where integrity may be lacking. Then, ask God, "Where
am I lacking integrity?" And allow him to shine his light
in the places of your life that need realignment to his character, nature, and plans.

Journal

Day 6:
Operating with Character

Dear Man of God,

When a woman thinks about a man with character, she considers the distinct characteristics that make you who you are—your mental, emotional, and ethical qualities. Building and nurturing strong character is vital to your journey as a man of God.

Character is not about wearing a mask or pretending to be someone you're not. It's about being true to you, embracing your individuality, and allowing God to shape and mold you into who He created you to be. When we show up in places and spaces in our true character, we allow people to make a decision about who we are and determine where we fit and also allow us to decide where they fit.

As men of God, you are called to follow the example of Christ and model His character. Jesus lived a life characterized by love, humility, integrity, strength, power, and selflessness. He showed us what it means to live a life that brings glory to God and blesses others.

Building character involves aligning our thoughts, attitudes, and actions with the teachings of Christ. It requires us to examine our hearts and seek transformation through the power of the Holy Spirit. We can study the words of Jesus, meditate on His teachings, and follow His example in our daily lives. May God bless you abundantly

Dear Man of God

as you reflect the character of Christ in all that you do.

SCRIPTURES:

Hebrews 6:12 and Galatians 5:22-23

Take time today to reflect on your character and ask God to reveal areas that need refinement. Then, find one scripture related to a place where you could use some growth and meditate on it as you conquer your day.

Journal

_____

_____

_____

_____

_____

_____

_____

_____

_____

_____

_____

_____

_____

_____

_____

_____

_____

_____

_____

_____

_____

_____

_____

_____

_____

Day 7:
Walking in Power and Boldness

Dear Man of God,

You will encounter many obstacles in this life. Some of the greatest obstacles any person will overcome are strongholds. Strongholds are not physical or tangible; they begin in the mind, rooted in our thoughts and beliefs. Dr. Clarence Walker defines strongholds as forceful stubborn arguments, rationales, opinions, ideas, or philosophies that resist the knowledge of Jesus Christ. Do not fear because there is hope. The great news is that you have the power as men of God, through the power of the Holy Spirit, to overcome them.

As followers of Christ, you must recognize and address these strongholds in your lives. They can manifest as hidden secrets, unhealthy habits, addictions, or negative thinking and behavioral patterns. However, God has given you the power and authority to overcome them through His Word and the resources He has provided.

Strongholds are similar to shadows. As a child, shadows appeared large, scary, and harmful. To make them disappear, someone would turn on a light and the shadows would disappear, or they would change its position to not appear as intimidating as they did. Shadows appear when an object is between you and the light source. Strongholds are designed to appear bigger and stronger than God. They appear larger, scarier, and more harmful when they are between you and the Light of the World, Jesus. Jesus has already defeated and overcame every stronghold. This means you are able to defeat them as well.

To overcome strongholds, you must first acknowledge the power and authority that God has given you. You are not powerless against these mental battles. As men of God, it is crucial to understand your weapons. Let me share with you what Dr. Benjamin Smith's acronym "WEAPONS" stands for:

W - The Word of God: The Scriptures are a powerful weapon that reveal the truth, bring transformation, and help us renew our minds.

E - Effective Prayer: Prayer is a vital tool that allows us to commune with God, seek His guidance, and receive His strength to overcome strongholds.

A - Armor of God: We are equipped with the armor of God, which includes the belt of truth, the breastplate of righteousness, the shield of faith, the helmet of salvation, the sword of the Spirit (which is the Word of God), and the shoes of peace. This armor protects and empowers us in spiritual warfare.

P - Promises of God: God's promises provide us with hope, assurance, and the confidence to overcome any stronghold. We can stand on His faithful promises and declare them over our lives.

Dear Man of God

O - Offerings of God: Our worship, obedience, and surrender to God are offerings that invite His presence and power into our lives. Through worship and obedience, we experience the breakthrough and deliverance from strongholds.

N - Name of God: The name of Jesus is mighty and carries authority. When we invoke the name of Jesus, strongholds must bow and flee. It is through His name that we have victory.

S - Spirit of God: The Holy Spirit dwells within us, empowering and guiding us. He is not a lesser version of God. He is our Helper, our Comforter, and the One who leads us into all truth. Relying on the Holy Spirit enables us to overcome strongholds.

You have been given the weapons to combat and overcome strongholds. Through the Word of God, effective prayer, the armor of God, the promises of God, your offerings to Him, the name of Jesus, and the presence of the Holy Spirit, you are empowered to walk in victory.

SCRIPTURE:
Deuteronomy Chapter 8:17-18 Luke 10:19, 2 Corinthians 10:4

Take time today to locate any strongholds that may be present in your life. Seek God's guidance and utilize the weapons He has given you to overcome them.

Journal

_____

_____

_____

_____

_____

_____

_____

_____

_____

_____

_____

_____

_____

_____

_____

_____

_____

_____

_____

_____

_____

_____

_____

_____

_____

_____

_____

Dear Man of God

Day 8:
Building Trust

Dear Man of God,

Trust is a precious and delicate thing. Building trust takes time and effort, yet it can be quickly shattered. The ultimate example of trustworthiness is the trustworthiness of our Heavenly Father, revealed through His Son, Jesus Christ.

God has shown Himself to be completely trustworthy throughout history. He has kept His promises, fulfilled His prophecies, and remained faithful to His Word. Even when it takes longer than we expect or understand, His faithfulness endures. We can trust Him wholeheartedly because He is a God who never lies.

I understand that if you have an absent or unreliable earthly father, it may be challenging to trust in the role of a heavenly Father. The wounds of broken trust run deep, but I want to encourage you to open your heart to the possibility of a trustworthy Father in God. One of the beautiful attributes of God is that He is not like man. So, no matter how others have treated you, rejoice that God is not like them.

Our heavenly Father is unlike any earthly father or person we may have encountered. He is loving, compassionate, and steadfast. His character is perfect, and His promises are true. He will never fail us or abandon us. Even in moments of doubt or uncertainty, He remains faithful. Even the most trustworthy person you can think of who never goes back on their word or fails to fulfill their obligations can't compare to the faithfulness of God.

I invite you to let down your guard and trust in Him. Release any preconceived notions or comparisons based on earthly experiences. Instead, anchor your trust in the unwavering character of God. Get to know him for who he is and not who others have been in your life. When you allow God to love you like no one ever has, you will find that he is far better than anyone could ever be.

SCRIPTURE:
Proverbs 3:5-6, Isaiah 26:3-4

Take time today to reflect on your trust in God. If there are areas where trust has been difficult for you, surrender them to Him and ask for His healing touch. Open your heart to the possibility of a trustworthy Heavenly Father who will never disappoint you. Choose to trust Him, knowing He is faithful to fulfill His promises.

.

Journal

Day 9:
Deconstructing Your Faith

Dear Man of God,

We commonly inherit limited and sometimes incorrect teachings from our family members or other trusted people concerning God, Jesus Christ, and our salvation. When our beliefs are confronted with the truth of God's Word, it can cause doubt and uncertainty to arise within us. This can require a journey of deconstruction and reconstruction of your faith.

Undoing the false narrative and truth ingrained within you throughout your life is similar to house flipping. A skilled house flipper can see a dilapidated structure and recognize its potential for transformation. They understand that in order to create something new and beautiful, the old must be stripped down, revealing a blank canvas for reconstruction. But the key to starting reconstruction on a house is to recognize that the old material isn't serving the house anymore.

Likewise, if you find yourself in a season of deconstructing your faith, it can be an excellent place to be. It is an opportunity to examine and dismantle the beliefs and practices that may have been forced upon you through tradition or religion. It is a chance to build a foundation of your belief rooted in a genuine, personal, and authentic relationship with the Creator of all mankind.

Moreover, deconstructing your faith can be an unsettling act. It causes you to question ideologies shared by trusted individuals. These individuals could be your parents or other trusted family members, childhood pastors, friends, teachers, coaches, or any other person you admire. Deconstruction will also cause you to question your identity–especially if you intertwine your beliefs to your culture. Although this process can produce pain, there is a purpose for this pain. This process will allow you to build an authentic and genuine relationship with Christ based on your personal experiences, not just those experiences shared with you by others.

However, deconstruction should never be an end in itself. It is vital to have a plan for reconstruction. As you uproot, tear down, and destroy the old constructs of your beliefs, it is essential to have a vision of what you want to rebuild. This vision should be based on the revelation of God's Word and the leading of the Holy Spirit.

In this process, you have the opportunity to establish a firsthand account of who God is and His purpose for your life. In addition, it is an invitation to intimately know the creator, not merely through the experiences or stories of others, but through your encounters with Him. Trust that He will transform and build something beautiful in your life through this process.

SCRIPTURES:
Jeremiah 1:10, Matthew 7:24-29

Take time today to reflect on your faith journey. Are there areas in your beliefs or practices that need to be deconstructed? First, seek the guidance of the Holy Spirit as you tear down old constructs. Then, create a vision for reconstructing your faith founded on the truth of God's Word and a genuine relationship with Him.

Journal

Day 10:
Reconstructing Your Faith

Dear Man of God,

Building your faith on a solid foundation—a foundation of acquired knowledge through seeking God is one of the most important things you can do. Like a great reporter or journalist, who asks questions, interviews, takes notes and checks the facts, you should approach your faith with a similar mindset.

Belief should not be based solely on blind acceptance but on evidence and truth. The Bible is a reliable source of evidence, providing a blueprint for building a new relationship with God, and living a transformed life.

When a reporter investigates a story, they gather information from credible sources. In our faith journey, we have access to the ultimate source of truth—God's Word. The Bible contains God's testimonies, teachings, and revelations, revealing His character, plans, and promises. It is a treasure chest of knowledge that we can explore and examine.

Just as a reporter fact-checks their sources, we should take the time to verify the truths presented in scripture. Seek God in prayer, study His Word, and allow the Holy Spirit to guide you into all truth. Take notes, ask questions, and wrestle with the teachings of the Bible. Through this process, you will deepen your understanding, gain fresh revelation and perspective, and develop a solid foundation for your faith.

SCRIPTURE:

Jeremiah 1:10, Matthew 7:25, Matthew 7:7

Take time today to reflect on the foundation of your faith. Are you building upon acquired knowledge or seeking God for a new personal revelation to reconstruct wrong perspectives or narratives? Write down areas that you don't have clarity about and seek God's knowledge.

Journal

Day 11:
Godly Leadership

Dear Man of God,

Godly leadership is grounded in humility and selflessness. It is not rooted in selfish ambition but in a sincere desire to seek wisdom, receive wise counsel, and surrender to the leading of the Holy Spirit. As a man of God, you have the privilege and responsibility to lead others with a heart that reflects the love and guidance of your Heavenly Father. Leading others isn't about being in control or in charge; it is about how much you can bring out the untapped greatness in other people.

Imagine walking in the woods with a child under your care. The child, in their curiosity, veers off the path and begins to explore the surrounding area. However, as their guardian, you call out their name, gently guiding them back to the right track. Though the grass may be high, you leave a path for them to follow. Because of the relationship you have built with the child, they recognize your voice and trust your guidance, knowing that your love for them will not lead them astray. This is a great example of how God leads us through life.

In the same way, as a leader, you have the opportunity to forge a path and make the way clearer for those who are following behind you. Therefore, your focus should not solely be on your desires or ambitions but on what is truly best for those under your care, whether it be your children, your team, or your company.

Authentic godly leadership involves sacrificial love. It requires you to set aside personal agendas and preferences, seek the guidance of the Holy Spirit, and prioritize the well-being and growth of those entrusted to your leadership. Your role is to nurture, guide, and protect those who look to you for direction.

One of the significant parts of leadership is that the leader is also being led; that is what makes a leader great. When you let the Holy Spirit lead you and instruct you throughout the day, he will help you to lead others. God knows what those you are leading need, and he knows how to bring the best out of them in the same way that he knows how to bring the best out of you.

SCRIPTURES:
1 Kings 3:10-12

Reflect on your leadership role and describe what attributes make you a great leader. Are you leading with godly intentions, focusing on the well-being of those entrusted to your care? Seek the wisdom and guidance of the Holy Spirit as you make decisions and interact with others. Remember that true leadership is not about personal gain but serving and nurturing those who follow.

May your leadership be marked by love, wisdom, and a deep commitment to the well-being of others, ultimately bringing glory to our Heavenly Father.

Journal

_____

_____

_____

_____

_____

_____

_____

_____

_____

_____

_____

_____

_____

_____

_____

_____

_____

_____

_____

_____

_____

_____

_____

_____

_____

_____

Day 12:
Forgiving Yourself

Dear Man of God,

No one knows you better than yourself. You see the good, the bad, and the ugly. We are all acquainted with the mistakes we've made, both big and small. We've all stumbled and caused pain, and while others may extend forgiveness and move on, it is often difficult for us to forgive ourselves. It's as if we find ourselves locked in a cage of unforgiveness, holding the key in our hands but refusing to turn it and set ourselves free.

Imagine being confined within a jail cell, the key to your release securely in your grasp. Yet, you remain imprisoned despite having the means to unlock the door and step into freedom. This is how it feels when you hold onto unforgiveness towards others and yourself. It hinders your ability to walk in the fullness of God's grace and prevents you from giving others the love and understanding they need and deserve from you.

But here's the truth: Christ has already forgiven you. He took the weight of your mistakes and sins upon Himself and offered you complete forgiveness through His sacrifice on Calvary's cross. When we hold things in, unwilling to let them go, it begins to damage us internally and wreak havoc in our lives and the lives of others. As a follower of Christ, you are called to mirror His example of forgiveness in your own life. You may have made mistakes, but Christ died even for those. Even the worst offense is covered by the blood of Christ. He offers us the gift of forgiveness, and with that forgiveness comes freedom, but it is our responsibility to accept it, forgive ourselves, and move forward.

Accept God's sacrifice, move forward as forgiven men of God in the light of His grace, extending forgiveness to yourselves and others along the way. May your life be a testament to His love and mercy.

SCRIPTURES:
Romans 3:23, Philippians 3:13, and Romans 8:1

Take a moment to reflect on any areas where you still hold onto unforgiveness towards yourself. Ask the Holy Spirit to help you. As you think about these things, write them down, whatever scenarios or memories arise. Once your list is finished, destroy it and declare yourself forgiven and free! Release those burdens to God and accept His forgiveness. Embrace the freedom He offers, knowing that He has redeemed your past and given you a future filled with hope.

Journal

_____

_____

_____

_____

_____

_____

_____

_____

_____

_____

_____

_____

_____

_____

_____

_____

_____

_____

_____

_____

_____

_____

_____

_____

_____

_____

_____

Day 13:
Finding Your Voice

Dear Man of God,

In a world that often values the opinions and reactions of men, you need to find your confidence and boldness in the assuredness that God is with you. When you focus on Him rather than on the faces and reactions of others, you can speak with courage and conviction. You need not worry about how people may respond or whether you have the same education, training, or background as those around you. Instead, your primary focus should be on Christ and His presence in your life.

Your voice is valuable! There are things you have experienced, wisdom you can contribute, and lessons you can share with the world to make it better than it was before. As men, protectors, and leaders in your families, your voices carry weight and influence. When you speak boldly, you become an example to those around you, especially young boys who look up to you. We live in a world void of truth and the love of God, and He wants to use your voice to make a difference. Man of God, use your voice to proclaim the truth, encourage others, speak life, give discipline in love, and share the wisdom you've gained from your relationship with Christ.

Speaking boldly does not mean you are free from fear. It is natural to experience fear, but you can still be bold even in the face of fear. When rooted in Christ, we can courageously speak up, lead, and boldly say what needs to be proclaimed.

I want to share a personal reflection from my own life as a wife. When I hear my husband's voice encouraging me, even when I am unsure or afraid, it brings a sense of calm and reassurance. His words empower me to face whatever challenges lie ahead. He may not realize how much his voice means to me and how it helps me navigate life's uncertainties, but whether he knows it or not, it is a source of power, strength, and reassurance for me.

Finding your confidence and boldness in Christ grants you the strength to speak the truth in love, knowing that your words can inspire and lead others. May the boldness of your voice reflect the power of God working within you, making a lasting impact on the lives of those you encounter.

SCRIPTURES:
Acts 4:29, 1 John 5:14, Proverbs 18:21

Have there been times where you needed to use your voice but have yet to? Think about the importance of speaking boldly, not out of arrogance or pride, but out of the profound assurance that comes from your relationship with Christ. When you second guess using your voice, determine where the desire to use your voice is coming from, and if it is rooted in Christ, then don't stifle his ability to use you. Use your voice!

Journal

Day 14:
Toxic Masculinity

Dear Man of God,

Your manhood is a gift from God, but if you don't become one with the nature of God, masculinity can become toxic. Society says men are fearless, strong, and don't show emotion, but that is false. Because when I look at the life of Christ, he was brave and strong, AND He also allowed himself to be vulnerable and show emotion.

Society has taught us that crying and displaying emotions are signs of weakness. As a result, men have built walls between their actions and ability to truly connect with others. I honestly believe men feel emotions deep within, but sometimes lack an outlet to express them because of a lingering fear of being perceived as weak.

Let's take an even closer look at the life of Jesus. He, too, experienced a wide range of emotions. He wept, cried, and even expressed anger so that he could be acquainted with our griefs and sorrows. Jesus showed us that it is not wrong to feel these emotions. They are a natural part of being human. We all need a safe place to share our feelings and give them a voice.

By suppressing your emotions, you inadvertently teach your children and those around you to do the same, creating barriers to building deep and meaningful relationships. You need to give a voice to your emotions so others can learn to do the same. You can't give your emotions a voice if you can't give them a name.

In times like these, I like to use an "emotion wheel." This wheel represents the vast array of feelings and emotions we experience. It goes beyond the basic categories of happiness, sadness, and anger. By acknowledging and embracing your emotions, you can connect with Christ deeper. He experienced these emotions Himself and understands what you are going through. May you find freedom and healing as you embrace the fullness of your emotions, knowing that Jesus walks beside you every step of the way.

SCRIPTURES:
John 11:35, Isaiah 53:3

Take some time to use the internet to search for an emotion wheel. Use it to detect how you have been feeling lately. Are you allowing yourself to feel and express your emotions in a healthy and godly manner? Do you feel safe enough to share your true emotions with others? Consider how emotional openness can impact your relationships, especially with your significant other, children, family, and friends. Take some time to write out your emotions, voice them, connect with Christ, and become a stronger, more compassionate man who reflects the heart of the Savior.

Journal

_____

_____

_____

_____

_____

_____

_____

_____

_____

_____

_____

_____

_____

_____

_____

_____

_____

_____

_____

_____

_____

_____

_____

_____

_____

_____

_____

_____

Dear Man of God

Day 15:
Your Identity is Not in Your Work

Dear Man of God,

We can spend so much time at our place of work or investing in what we do that we can begin to identify ourselves by what we do. But, you may be asking, what is wrong with that? If you are what you do, what happens when you aren't doing it anymore or if you don't do a good job one day? You relate your work to your worth, and one has nothing to do with the other. In our Western culture, what we do for a living often becomes a measure of our status and worth. However, I want to remind you that this is not the basis of Christ's love for you.

Christ's love for you is not dependent on your occupation or accomplishments. He loves you simply because you are His creation. Your work or social status does not determine your value in His eyes. It is not about working your way into righteousness or earning your place in heaven. Instead, Christ's love for you is unconditional and stems from your belief in Him and your love for Him.

You inadvertently limit yourself when you tie your identity solely to your work. You miss building intimate relationships, finding rest, and experiencing the fullness of life God intends for you. There is so much more to life than work and how many plaques, certificates, and degrees you can hang on the wall. There needs to be a balance. Work should not define who you are or become your sole (and soul) identity. What you do is a tool for God to develop you and to impact the lives of others. God places you in specific roles because you are valuable to what you are called to, not because what you are called to determines your value.

Find your identity and worth in your relationship with Christ. It is, through Him, that you discover your true purpose and fulfillment. Your value lies in being a child of God, not in the titles or positions you hold. God helps you to find your identity and gives you a revelation of who you are as his beloved child. The Bible shares a plethora of God's thoughts concerning you as His child. He teaches you how to value yourself, as He does, and others through His word and the example of Christ. May you find peace and joy in knowing that you are loved by the Creator of the universe, regardless of your occupation or societal status.

SCRIPTURES:
Psalm 139:14, Ephesians 2:10, Isaiah 64:6

Take some time today and think about how you view your own identity. Are you placing too much emphasis on your work or what you do for a living? Take an honest inventory of your life and think if you have tied your identity to your work, hobby, etc. Consider the areas where you may need to find balance and prioritize your relationship with Christ and the people around you.

Journal

_____

_____

_____

_____

_____

_____

_____

_____

_____

_____

_____

_____

_____

_____

_____

_____

_____

_____

_____

_____

_____

_____

_____

_____

_____

_____

_____

Day 16:
Know Your Value

Dear Man of God,

In this age of social media, there is a great temptation to compare ourselves to others and to desire what they have. It's easy to get caught up in the highlight reels and carefully curated images we see online without considering the backstories or the reality behind those pictures. Unfortunately, not only is the grass not greener, but in many of these scenarios, the grass isn't even real.

Comparison is indeed a thief of joy. When you constantly compare yourself to others, you diminish your worth and value and count what they have as superior to who God created you to be and what He has for you. You lose sight of who you are and why you were created. You begin to believe your worth is determined by what you have or how you measure up to others. That is a lie from our enemy. You, Man of God, are enough!

Moreover, I want to remind you worldly possessions or achievements do not define your worth and value. Instead, your worth is found in your identity as a beloved child of God. When you understand this truth, you can appreciate, be content, and value what you have been entrusted with despite what others post or do.

Let me share a powerful example. There was a woman who seemed to have it all. She posted pictures with designer bags, appearing to take luxurious vacations every week. People envied her and compared themselves to her often. She had many online followers on all of the social media platforms. Several people even posted they felt their lives were so far behind because they could not compare to the extravagant life she was living. However, when invited to a national conference to be a guest panelist, she shared the truth with the conference organizer. To their surprise, she had just been evicted and was living on her friend's couch, uncertain about her future. She wasn't sure if she would have enough funds to purchase the necessary flight to get to the conference. Her social 'life' was, in fact, a lie!

This story reminds us that what we see on the surface is often not the whole truth. We miss the deeper reality when we compare ourselves to others based on outward appearances. As a result, we become discontented and may even seek material possessions and worldly achievements rather than a genuine relationship with God and others in our lives.

True contentment comes from knowing who we are in Christ and stewarding what we have been given well. It is finding joy in our blessings rather than constantly yearning for more. When you continually search for more, you will never realize you have exactly what you need. When we chase after God's heart rather than His hand or what is in the hand of others, you experience a deeper and more meaningful relationship with Him.

SCRIPTURES:

2 Corinthians 10:12, 1 Thessalonians 4:11-12, James 3:16, 1 John 2:15

Please note your time on social media and how it has affected you. Taking a break from social media platforms is okay to connect with God and yourself. Make sure you are spending more time meditating on what God has said concerning your life than on what is happening in the lives of others.

Journal

Day 17:
Being a Kingdom Citizen

Dear Man of God,

Did you know you have incredible benefits and rights as a citizen of God's Kingdom? Yes, sir, you actually do. Understanding what it means to be a king in God's Kingdom changes how you live and operate in this world.

As a citizen of God's Kingdom, you are not just a mere mortal living out your days on earth. You are a spiritual being, placed here for a purpose and a set amount of time. Therefore, it is crucial to grasp the significance of our identity as a kingdom citizen and the privileges that come with it. If you don't, you can become subject to the ways and circumstances of a world that you were meant to impact, not to be impacted by.

In human kingdoms, there are certain rights and privileges that citizens enjoy. For example, in the earthly kingdom of Britain, the queen has the power to gift islands in the Bahamas to individuals because they are outposts of the British kingdom. Similarly, as kingdom citizens, you operate under the power and authority of our King, God Himself.

Being a citizen of God's Kingdom means that you don't speak on your own accord; you speak on behalf of the King. You carry His authority and represent Him in this world. Just as a king has the final say and whatever he decrees becomes the law, our King, God, has the ultimate authority over everything and enforces that authority through us.

As a kingdom citizen, you have the privilege of experiencing God's forgiveness, healing, redemption, and restoration. Your King extends His love and compassion to you, supplying your needs, and satisfying your deepest desires with good things. He renews your strength and gives you the ability to soar like an eagle. You don't have to wait until you get to heaven to experience the benefits of being a child of God. You carry them with you as an heir of his kingdom and can use our kingdom's jurisdiction to change circumstances, mindsets, and surroundings. May you experience the fullness of God's blessings as you live as a kingdom citizen.

SCRIPTURES:
John 15:16, Genesis 1:27, Philippians 3:20 1 Peter 1:3-4

Take some time to meditate on the scriptures and let God illuminate to you what it means to be a kingdom citizen, and with that revelation, discover areas of your life where you can use your kingdom standing with God to make a difference.

Journal

_____

_____

_____

_____

_____

_____

_____

_____

_____

_____

_____

_____

_____

_____

_____

_____

_____

_____

_____

_____

_____

_____

_____

_____

Dear Man of God

Day 18:
Leaving an Inheritance

Dear Man of God,

What will people say about you when you're no longer here? What do you want to be remembered for? I want to challenge you to consider the inheritance you are leaving behind. It goes beyond material wealth and possessions–it's much bigger than that. It is about the integrity of your character, the way you walk in love and kindness, and the impact you have on those around you. We have been taught to watch what we say, but people are more impacted by our lives than our words. People may not remember your name, but they will always remember how you made them feel when they were in your presence.

In Galatians 5:22-23, we are reminded of the fruit of the Spirit: love, joy, peace, patience, kindness, goodness, faithfulness, gentleness, and self-control. These are the qualities that should mark your life as a follower of Christ. They are the true indicators of a life lived with integrity, purpose, and impact.

Think about what you want to impart to others. We are all imparting something to someone, and we can decide what that is. My grandfather left me an inheritance and impartation of his character. He was a man of peace, known for his wisdom and ability to bring calmness to turbulent situations. People respected and sought him for wisdom because he lived a life guided by the Spirit.

Consider your impact on others, even in ways you may not know. Sometimes, we fail to recognize the value we bring to people's lives. Please take time to ask your inner circle about the qualities they see in you, the impact you make, and the legacy you are leaving behind. Their insights may surprise you and clarify the unique strengths and virtues that define you.

Be intentional about your work to shape your character and influence. Seek the values and virtues that align with God's heart and purpose for your life.

Remember, this journey is not about accumulating possessions or striving for self gain. It is about walking in the footsteps of our Savior, Jesus Christ, and leaving a lasting inheritance of love, kindness, and integrity. It is about becoming more like Him and reflecting His character to the world. And when you do, the other things will be added to your life!

SCRIPTURES:
Proverbs 13:22, Galatians 5:22-23, Matthew 6:33

Take some time to think about some of the things you wish someone taught you, showed you, or left you, and think about how you can share the same things with people you know. I encourage you to be intentional about the inheritance you are giving to others as you seek to embody the fruit of the Spirit in all aspects of your life.

Journal

_____

_____

_____

_____

_____

_____

_____

_____

_____

_____

_____

_____

_____

_____

_____

_____

_____

_____

_____

_____

_____

_____

_____

_____

Day 19:
What is Your Legacy?

Dear Man of God,

Today, I encourage you to think about the legacy you are leaving behind. What mark will you leave on this world when you are long gone? Will you have an impact that outlives you? How will your family and friends remember you? It's not just about the present moment but about your lasting impact on future generations.

As men of God, you are called to think beyond your lifetimes. You serve a God who is concerned with the generations to come. Therefore, you are called to build something that will outlast you and bring honor to God and bless future generations. This legacy is not limited to financial inheritance but encompasses the values and principles you pass down to your children.

Consider the example of Abraham in the Bible. He was known as a man of faith who walked in obedience to receive God's promises. He even left his family of idol worshippers to follow God's plan for his life. His legacy extended far beyond his lifetime, as he became the father of many nations and a spiritual ancestor to believers throughout history. From the time God spoke to Abraham about having a child, he spoke of the generations to come because in each of us is the ability to influence and impact generations even after we are gone.

When we have a plan or a vision that begins or ends

with us, it should be an automatic indicator that we are not thinking big enough. God is a big thinker who gives you visions that extend beyond your own reach and abilities, so you need Him to fulfill the vision. God makes the vision grand enough to impact other people's lives for generations to come.

God has already designed the plan on how He can get your wisdom, talents, and ideas to the next generation. You just have to be open to receiving God's heart for you knowing that there are lives that God has attached to the fulfillment of your purpose. Lives that extend beyond your family, friend circle, and those you may know. There are people who you may never meet in your life that God desires to use you to impact.

Your reach is only limited when you do not bring God into your plans and stunt what He wants to do in your life by thinking one-dimensionally instead of generationally. There is great work to be done, and He wants to use you to do it. Will you allow Him to impact generations through you?

SCRIPTURES:
Proverbs 13:22 Ecclesiastes 2:26

What stamp do you want to leave on the world for future generations? Are you intentionally investing your time, energy, and resources into building something that will outlast you? If you have yet to think about this, it is never too early or too late. Someone in future generations needs what you have; how will you get it to them? Write down the thoughts that come to mind as you answer these questions and allow God to guide you into leaving a legacy that honors him.

Journal

_____

_____

_____

_____

_____

_____

_____

_____

_____

_____

_____

_____

_____

_____

_____

_____

_____

_____

_____

_____

_____

_____

_____

_____

Day 20:
Safety and Provision

Dear Man of God,

Safety is important in our lives. The term "safety" is multidimensional. It involves many aspects: emotional, physical, financial, and spiritual safety. As a woman speaking to a man, I want you to understand the significance of these aspects in building strong relationships.

We have touched on this, but the first area is emotional safety. It means creating an environment where vulnerability is not weaponized but embraced and where others will not use your vulnerability against you. Both women and men must open up and share their emotions without fear or judgment. We all need a safe place to exist without shrewdness or dread. As men, you must recognize that emotional strength is not about suppressing your feelings but acknowledging and expressing them in a healthy way to people you trust.

Secondly, physical safety is something women and children often seek in men. Your families will consider you a source of protection and security. Women desire to feel safe in your presence just as our Heavenly Father is our ultimate refuge. It means being physically strong, aware, and willing to protect your loved ones.

Furthermore, financial safety is often associated with men's roles as providers. While financial stability is essential, it should not overshadow the need for emotional availability. Women seek not only financial security but also emotional support and connection. It brings you to a place of peace when you can find a balance and prioritize nurturing healthy relationships over solely focusing on financial responsibilities.

Lastly, spiritual safety is significant in your walk with God. As men of God, you are responsible for spiritually leading your families. It means creating an atmosphere where faith can thrive, your loved ones can find solace, and your children can grow in their relationship with God. So strive to be a man who provides emotional, physical, financial, and spiritual security, embracing vulnerability and understanding and creating an environment where your loved ones can find safety and peace.

SCRIPTURES:
Proverbs 18:10 Genesis 2:25

Write down the different ways you provide safety and how you are helping your loved ones to feel safe in those areas through your actions. If there are any areas you aren't providing a safe place, ask God to help you and show you how to become a safe place for your loved ones.

Journal

_____

_____

_____

_____

_____

_____

_____

_____

_____

_____

_____

_____

_____

_____

_____

_____

_____

_____

_____

_____

_____

_____

_____

_____

_____

_____

_____

_____

Dear Man of God

Day 21:
Friendship and Close Relationships

Dear Man of God,

Relationships were given to us by God for several reasons, but mainly because we can't do life without the help of others. King Solomon, one of the wisest men that ever lived, told us that two are better than one. We were created for community–not isolation. God is a people-centered God. He utilizes people to fulfill His will on the earth. God spoke to Himself and said it isn't good for man to be by himself. Every now and then, it is good to take inventory of those you have close to you and ensure they are assets to your life and not liabilities.

Someone who is considered an asset to your life will add value, in the form of wisdom, advice, encouragement, discipline, and peace. Are you surrounded by people with wise counsel? It is dangerous to have only 'yes' men in your inner circle. True wisdom comes from seeking the counsel of those who are grounded in God's Word and have your best interests at heart, even if it hurts your feelings. If everyone you know is only seeking you for advice but never has any to offer, it may mean that you could use some new friends in your circle.

Accountability plays a significant role in this aspect. A genuine friend will not only support you but also hold you accountable. They will have the courage to speak the truth into your life, even if it is not what you want to hear at the time. Their words may be challenging but necessary for your growth and protection. One of the best indicators of love in relationships is one's willingness to tell you the truth and hold you accountable for your words and actions.

It is vital to have people who are not afraid to tell you the truth in love, even if it hurts. The truth without love can be reckless and harmful. A true friend will consider your future more than your present feelings, seeking your well-being above all else. May your relationships be marked by a healthy balance of support and accountability, encouragement and discipline, love and life. And may you continue to seek wisdom from those who will challenge and uplift you on your faith journey.

SCRIPTURES:
Proverbs 27:5-6, Ecclesiastes 4:9-12

I encourage you to evaluate the company you keep. Write down the qualities that you find important in relationships and take an inventory of your friends. If they lack some qualities necessary in friendship, ask God to surround you with wise counsel—those who will hold you accountable and guide you according to God's Word, for friendships are built on truth, love, and understanding.

Dear Man of God

Journal

Day 22:
Mission, Vision & Values

Dear Man of God,

It is amazing to me that the top companies and corporations in the world will spend millions of dollars and countless hours to ensure they have effective mission, vision, and value statements. This must mean these concepts are important. These statements are the foundational components of their businesses and are the driving forces of their productivity. Amid all your responsibilities, spend time on things that align with your mission and vision. We must understand the meaning and purpose behind our actions in our personal lives and relationships.

Let's define what mission and vision mean. Our mission is the overarching purpose that guides our decisions and actions. It is the reason we exist and the ultimate goal we strive to achieve. On the other hand, our vision is the specific picture of our desired future. It gives us direction and clarity, allowing us to make choices that align with our purpose. It answers that question, "How do I know I've achieved this thing?".

In the context of marriage, both partners need to understand and embrace the mission and vision of their union. When you have a shared understanding of where and why you are together, you can face challenges with unity and harmony. Instead of fighting against each other, you fight for each other. You will work together to overcome obstacles because your focus is on the greater mission. It combats the selfishness we have to focus on the collective goal and purpose of the marriage. In this context, the investment in your marriage should be more than the investment in your wedding day.

It can be easy to elevate one vision over another in marriage. This is contrary to the idea of submission in the context of marriage, and subsequently, why people balk at the idea of submission. Submission within marriage is not about one person being superior to the other but rather about aligning personal missions with the mission of the marriage. It is a willingness to surrender your individual goals and desires to the greater purpose of your union. Doing so creates a solid foundation for your relationship's growth, love, and support.

Just as top organizations invest significant resources in defining their mission, vision, and values, you, too, must be intentional about knowing your own. Discover the mission, vision, and values for your life and relationships. Understand where you are going and why it matters. This knowledge will empower you to make decisions aligned with your purpose and to prioritize your time and energy accordingly.

Knowing the value of your "yes" and "no" becomes easier when you have a clear mission and vision. Then, you can confidently say "yes" to the opportunities and pursuits that align with your purpose and graciously say "no" to those that do not.

Habakkuk 2:2 1 Peter 5:6 Luke 22:42

Take time to reflect on your mission, vision, and values. What is the why behind what you do, and what is your vision for your life? Then put your mission and vision somewhere you can see it. This can be a list, a vision board, or a document. Wherever you put it, make sure you look at it often to remind yourself of the mission and vision and to stay the course when times get tough as you seek God's guidance and wisdom as you align your life with His purpose.

Journal

_____

_____

_____

_____

_____

_____

_____

_____

_____

_____

_____

_____

_____

_____

_____

_____

_____

_____

_____

_____

_____

_____

_____

_____

_____

_____

_____

_____

Day 23:
The Power of Impact

Dear Man of God,

Don't settle for a mundane life. Instead, God has called you to live purposefully and passionately, positively impacting the world around you. He called us to live an abundant life in Him–this is why Jesus came to the world.

In the Bible, salt is often used as a metaphor for your role as a follower of Christ. In ancient times, salt was not only used as seasoning for food but also for preservation, healing, and even as a currency. Just as salt adds flavor and enhances the taste of food, you are called to bring flavor and richness to the lives of others through your words, actions, and example.

When you dine at a restaurant and the food lacks taste, what's the first thing you grab? That's right, you go for the salt. Similarly, in a world that can sometimes feel dull and lifeless, you are called to be the salt that brings out the best in every situation. Your life should inspire others to rise above mediocrity and embrace their full potential in Christ.

Sometimes people think being a Christian means having a dull, mundane life, but that could not be further from the truth. Nothing is more exciting and adventurous than following Christ and allowing God to use you and your life to fulfill his earthly plans. God will take you places and give you experiences that you could never have imagined for yourself, and through the enjoyment of your own life, others will see the extraordinarily abundant lives they were meant to live in Christ.

We can't be salt to the world if we are not salt to begin with. You were made to have purpose and significance and live a life that radiates God, who is far from dull and average. We must see men living their lives to the fullest and becoming everything they are called to be in Christ. The world wants us to have imagery of men in a negative light. It's time that we see men as the glorious creations that they are. Living out full, impactful, influential, and inspiring lives, using their gifts and talents to spread the gospel of Christ. We need men living life fully, with joy and without apology. May your life inspire others to go beyond the ordinary and embrace their God-given potential.

SCRIPTURES:
Matthew 5:13-16 Ephesians 2:10

Are you impacting others in your life? What would it look like to have a meaningful life? Write down your thoughts because a meaningful life is an impactful life.

Journal

_____

_____

_____

_____

_____

_____

_____

_____

_____

_____

_____

_____

_____

_____

_____

_____

_____

_____

_____

_____

_____

_____

_____

_____

_____

Dear Man of God

Day 24:
Don't Quit

Dear Man of God,

Can I share a powerful scripture that has been a guiding light in my life: Ephesians 6:8-9. It says, "Knowing that whatsoever good thing any man doeth, the same shall he receive of the Lord, whether he be bound or free. And masters, treat your slaves in the same way. Do not threaten them since you know that he who is both their Master and yours is in heaven, and there is no favoritism with him."

At first glance, this verse may seem specific to the relationship between masters and slaves. However, if we delve deeper, we can uncover a timeless truth that applies to all our lives.

Life is filled with challenges and setbacks. There will be moments when it seems like doing what is right, honorable, and aligned with our purpose is not producing the desired results. It can be disheartening and tempting to give up, to compromise our values, or to take matters into our own hands.

But here's the encouragement I want to offer you today! Keep going and doing right, even when it feels like it's not working. Why? Because your ultimate Master, the One who sees and knows all, is in heaven, and He is the one who truly matters. He is not swayed by favoritism or external circumstances. Instead, he sees the faithfulness of your heart and the integrity of your actions and will reward you accordingly.

When you stay committed to doing what is right, regardless of the outcomes you may be experiencing, you are aligning yourself with God's divine purposes. You are living a life of obedience and surrender, trusting that He will work all things together for your good and His glory.

Remember the story of Joseph in the Old Testament. Despite facing numerous trials and setbacks, including being sold into slavery and unjustly imprisoned, Joseph remained faithful to God. God's divine plan was revealed, and Joseph was elevated to significant influence and impact.

In your journey as a man of God, there will be times when you may feel unseen, unheard, or undervalued. But take heart, for God sees your faithfulness. He sees your commitment to righteousness, integrity, and living according to His Word. Your labor in His Kingdom is never in vain. Trust in His timing, wisdom, and His plan for your life.

SCRIPTURES:
Galatians 6:9

What is the scripture that helps you to keep pushing when times get tough? If you don't have one, I encourage you to find a scripture you can meditate on when life gets challenging to remind you to keep going because you have a Father in heaven who is watching and rewarding you.

Journal

Day 25:
The Importance of Worship

Dear Man of God,

I love gospel music–all types and all genres. However, I had to learn that worship is not just a physical act or a mere routine; it's a posture of your heart. Worship is not a moment in a Christian church service with slow music and tears. When we genuinely understand the authority and power of God, worship becomes a lifestyle—a continuous outpouring of our affection and adoration towards Him.

In the book of Psalms, we find countless expressions of worship. David, a man after God's heart, understood the significance of worship and its rightful place in our lives. Psalm 95:6 says, "Come, let us bow down in worship; let us kneel before the Lord our Maker."

Worship is not limited to a particular moment. It goes beyond that. It is about recognizing the object of our affection, directing our hearts, thoughts, and words toward the one true God, and surrendering our lives to His lordship. It is presenting Him with the big and the small things. It is thanking Him in and for every situation in our lives. It is acknowledging Him in all we do.

In your journey as a man of God, you want to examine where you direct your affections. Are you worshiping God wholeheartedly, or have you unknowingly made idols of other things? Our affections easily drift toward worldly pursuits, material possessions, particular people, or even our achievements. We must be vigilant and mindful of where we place our ultimate devotion.

Jesus reminds us in Matthew 22:37-38, "Love the Lord your God with all your heart, soul, and mind. This is the first and greatest commandment." Our worship should flow from a deep love for God, a love that permeates every aspect of our being. We should worship in spirit and truth. That means even when we don't feel like it, we should. I would like to compare it with exercise–there are days I do not want to wake up early and do cardio. But I know the benefits of exercising to my physical, mental, and emotional health. So, I do it. I would encourage you to have the same affection toward worship. Just do it.

As we surrender our hearts in worship, we experience the transformational power of God's presence. It is in worship that we encounter His love, His grace, and His overwhelming goodness. We lay down our desires and preferences, acknowledging His sovereignty over our lives. In return, God reveals Himself profoundly, filling us with a renewed sense of purpose and fulfillment.

SCRIPTURES:
John 4:24, Psalms 75:1, Jerimiah 20:13

Think about your day; how often do you find yourself thinking about the goodness of God and allowing your thoughts to be filled with him? If it is not often or you are unsure, be more intentional and take breaks throughout the day to meditate on God and his goodness as an act of worship. It will not only transform your day, but it will fill you with a peace that only he can give.

Journal

Day 26:
The Issue of Pride

Dear Man of God,

There is a fine line between confidence and arrogance. And that fine line, Man of God, is called pride. We must understand this distinction because it directly impacts our relationship with God and those around us.

Pride puts us at the center, exalting our abilities and achievements above everything else. It elevates us to a position of authority, taking the place that rightfully belongs to God alone.

Pride can also manifest as arrogance in the refusal to seek help when needed. It is an unwillingness to acknowledge our limitations and dependence on others. When we become self-reliant and neglect to ask for assistance when we really need it, we operate with and in a spirit of pride.

Haughtiness is a clear indicator of pride. It reflects an inflated sense of self-importance and a disregard for the contributions of others. When we attribute our success solely to our efforts, we rob God of His glory and fail to recognize the blessings and opportunities He has bestowed on us.

Confidence, on the other hand, stems from a deep understanding of our identity in Christ. It is having faith in the gifts and abilities that God has placed within us. But crucially, it is also recognizing that these talents are not self-made. We acknowledge that every good and perfect gift comes from above. Our confidence rests not in our strength but in the power of God working through us.

When we walk confidently, we express gratitude to God for His grace and guidance. We recognize that any achievements or successes we experience are the results of His favor and provision. We give honor and glory to God, understanding that He is the source of our abilities and the One who deserves our praise.

SCRIPTURES:
Proverbs 11:2 Proverbs 6:16-19

Are there any areas of your life where you are uncoachable or unwilling to listen to others? These may be areas of pride. Ask God to reveal the places in your life where you are operating in pride and allow him to help you become humble in these areas.

Journal

_____

_____

_____

_____

_____

_____

_____

_____

_____

_____

_____

_____

_____

_____

_____

_____

_____

_____

_____

_____

_____

_____

_____

_____

_____

_____

Dear Man of God

Day 27:
The Importance of Being Healed

Dear Man of God,

Everyone has places of hurt and pain from their past experiences, but God wants to heal them. When you neglect your healing, you risk causing harm to yourself and others, unknowingly bleeding on those who did not cut you.

The saying "hurt people hurt people" carries great truth. Whether intentional or not, your pain and wounds can manifest in your actions and interactions with others. You may react out of the hurt you experienced at the age when the trauma occurred. It is as if you respond as the wounded child you once were, carrying the weight of those past experiences.

As men, you should acknowledge and admit that you have wounds. This admission does not diminish your worth as a Christian or a man; it is the first step toward complete healing. You must come before God with vulnerability and honesty, acknowledging your pain and seeking His guidance for healing.

Opening up to God about your wounds is an act of trust and surrender. It is an invitation for His healing power to work in your life. God longs to bring restoration and wholeness to every area of your being. He is your compassionate and loving Father who understands your pain and desires to see you healed.

Taking time to heal is an act of courage and strength that produces a healthier you and healthier relationships. It is a ripple effect in your life and relationships. It demands that you confront your pain, face your past, and allow God's healing touch to transform you from the inside out. Through the process of healing, you can experience the freedom and wholeness that God desires for you. May you find comfort and strength in God's presence as you embark on the path of healing, experiencing the abundant life that Christ came to give, being liberated from the pain of the past, and walking in the fullness of His joy.

SCRIPTURES:
1 Corinthians 13:11 Isaiah 53:5 3 John 1-2

I encourage you to prioritize your healing journey. Where do you need to experience healing? Don't shy away from it. Give God full access to your heart and write down what hurts. Where is the pain? Allow God to help you locate your hurt to bring healing and freedom.

Journal

_____

_____

_____

_____

_____

_____

_____

_____

_____

_____

_____

_____

_____

_____

_____

_____

_____

_____

_____

_____

_____

_____

_____

_____

Day 28:
Submitting to God

Dear Man of God,

Submission is a word that can be looked down upon because many need clarification on what actual submission means, why it is necessary, or where it starts. Submission is a kingdom principle, and it starts with submission to God. It is a topic that may seem challenging to grasp, but it holds great significance in our understanding of our identity and authority in God's kingdom.

Submission does not equate to weakness; instead, it is a demonstration of our recognition of the power and authority of the King. When we submit to God, we acknowledge His sovereignty and rightful place as our ultimate authority. It is an act of humility and reverence, aligning our will with His divine purposes.

Jesus often spoke about the kingdom of God and the kingdom of heaven. He emphasized the importance of aligning ourselves with the values and principles of His kingdom. We advance His kingdom on earth by submitting to God's authority and living in obedience to His Word.

Submission is not a passive surrender but an active engagement with the King and His purposes. As we submit to God, we invite His guidance, wisdom, and power to flow through us. We become vessels through which His kingdom is established, and His will is done.

As you embrace the concept of submission as a kingdom citizen and recognize the authority of the King in your life and yield your will to His, it will allow His love, grace, and wisdom to guide your decisions and actions. You will begin to walk in the confidence that comes from knowing you are a citizen of His kingdom, with the rights and authorities that accompany it.

In your submission to God, you will discover true strength and fulfillment. So trust in His goodness and sovereignty, and let His kingdom reign in every aspect of your life.

SCRIPTURES:
Matthew 4:23, Matthew 6:9-13 Romans 14:17-20

What are your thoughts on submission before reading the devotional today? Has your idea of submission changed? If so, how and what are some steps you can take to stay submitted to God?

Journal

_____

_____

_____

- -

_____

_____

_____

_____

_____

_____

_____

_____

_____

_____

_____

_____

_____

_____

_____

_____

_____

_____

_____

_____

_____

Dear Man of God

Day 29:
Persist Through the Pain

Dear Man of God,

To thrive in this life, you must learn to persist through pain. A song I like talks about this; here are some powerful lyrics of a song by Twila Paris called "The Warrior Is a Child." These words capture the essence of our journey as warriors in God's kingdom and the reality of facing challenges, pain, and weariness along the way.

In the song, this verse resonates deeply: "Unafraid because his armor is the best, but even soldiers need a quiet place to rest." As men of God, you will find strength in your faith and the armor of God that equips you for spiritual battles. You can march forward fearlessly, trusting in the protection and power of your heavenly Father. However, even the bravest warriors need moments of rest and restoration. These soldiers need a place and time of respite to be rejuvenated for the battle.

It is important to acknowledge that, despite your courage, you will also face struggles and pain. The lyrics continue, "People say that I am amazing, never face retreat, but they don't see the enemies that lay me at His feet." You may be perceived as solid and unwavering in your faith, but you encounter battles that are unseen by others. This is why you must bring your burdens, hurts, and disappointments to the feet of Jesus, seeking His solace and guidance.

As followers of Christ, you are not exempt from pain,

heartache, or life's challenges. You live in a fallen world where suffering exists. However, what sets you apart is your relationship with your loving Savior and the hope you have in Him. There is hope!

The Scriptures remind us of the importance of having a heart of flesh. A heart of flesh means we have the capacity to feel and be sensitive to the things of God and the struggles others face. It is a tender and compassionate heart that mirrors the heart of our Heavenly Father. But, on the other hand, a heart of stone represents a life devoid of love and empathy. It represents a calloused heart with layers of pain and hurt.

Your faith in Jesus gives you the courage to face your wounds and extend compassion to others who are hurting. It is in those moments of vulnerability and authenticity that you experience the depth of God's love and find the strength to continue on your journey.

SCRIPTURE:
Ezekiel 11:13

Do you sometimes find it challenging to keep going when life seems complicated? You persist through pain by allowing Jesus to bear it for you. Get in the practice of giving the areas of life that cause you stress, pain, hurt, or frustration to God. When you feel overwhelmed by life, write down what is causing you to feel that way, give it to God in prayer, and go forward knowing he is taking care of you and all things that concern you.

Journal

Day 30:
The Ability to Give and Receive

Dear Man of God,

As a man and leader of the home, it can be difficult receiving help, support, encouragement, and even gifts from others. It is often easier to give than to receive, but it is essential to understand the importance and strength found in the act of receiving.

The concept of receiving makes me think about the bible, where Jesus blew on the disciples and told them to receive the Holy Spirit. Receiving the Holy Spirit may have felt vulnerable, but it was a moment of great significance and strength. It marked the indwelling of God's power and presence within them.

Similarly, in our lives, there are times when we are called to receive. It may be receiving love, compliments, acts of kindness, or even help from others. However, opening ourselves up and accepting these things can be challenging. We may mistakenly believe that receiving makes us weak or dependent on others. But the truth is, it takes strength and humility to receive with an open heart.

Imagine getting a gift from someone. The gift remains unopened until you choose to receive it. Similarly, when people want to give you love, encouragement, or support, you must be open enough to receive it. In receiving, we acknowledge the value and worth of the giver's intention and extend gratitude.

Moreover, in our relationship with God, receiving plays a vital role. The Scriptures remind us that we are children of God, loved by Him. He promises to give us good gifts according to His will when we ask. Yet, sometimes we struggle to ask, receive, and fully embrace what God wants to provide us with. This could be because you feel unworthy or hesitate to let down your guard.

Letting down your guard and embracing the love, blessings, and provisions God and others want to pour into your life is okay. Receiving reflects humility, trust, and openness to the goodness of God and the people he uses. Allow yourself to be vulnerable and accept the help, support, encouragement, and love that others want to extend to you. Embrace the blessings and provisions that God has in store for you.

SCRIPTURES:
Mark 11:24 John 16:24

Are you a receiver? Is there anything you struggle to receive from others (help, advice, support, etc.)? Ask God to show you why you struggle to receive in that area and to heal you so that your heart can be open to all God has for you.

Journal

_____

_____

_____

_____

_____

_____

_____

_____

_____

_____

_____

_____

_____

_____

_____

_____

_____

_____

_____

_____

_____

_____

_____

_____

_____

Dear Man of God

Day 31:
A Father Who Cares

Dear Man of God,

As we close this devotional, I want to affirm and remind you of a profound truth that resonates within the depths of every man's soul: God's eternal and unwavering love for you. This truth is vital, especially for those who have experienced difficulty in connecting with and understanding God due to their relationship with their earthly father or father figure.

God's love surpasses human limitations, flaws, and imperfections. But, unfortunately, there have been instances where people, driven by personal agendas or unhealed heaArts, have misrepresented God, tarnishing His image in the eyes of others. This can create barriers and hinder your ability to embrace His love fully.

But hear this: God's love for you is eternal and internal. It surpasses any human understanding or experience. His love is unchanging, steadfast, and without conditions. It is not based on your performance, achievements, or relationship with your earthly Father. Instead, God's love for you is rooted in His nature and extends beyond earthly limitations.

Whatever wounds or scars you may carry from your past, God desires to heal and restore your heart. He longs to reveal His true nature and draw you into a deep, intimate relationship with Him. He wants you to know that you are His beloved son, cherished and valued beyond measure. He sees you, knows you intimately, and loves you completely. He is always ready to welcome you with open arms, guide, comfort, and empower you to live a life that reflects His love.

SCRIPTURES:
John 3:16

Take a moment to reflect on God's incredible love for you. Write down how God has revealed his love to you, and allow yourself to be enveloped by His eternal love. Let go of any misconceptions or preconceived notions hindering your connection with Him. Embrace the truth that your Heavenly Father deeply loves, accepts, and desires you.

Journal